WALKING WITH JESUS

WALKING WITH JESUS

How to Experience the Heart of the Bible

Taught by Neville Goddard

Part of the
NEVILLE EXPLAINS THE BIBLE
Series

For more information visit:
www.radicalcounselor.com

The ideas, concepts, and opinions expressed in this book are intended to be used for educational purposes only. This book is made available with the understanding that the author and publisher are not presenting any specific medical or psychological advice. The author and publisher claim no responsibility to any person or entity for any liability, loss, or damage caused or alleged to be caused directly or indirectly as a result of the use, application, or interpretation of the material in this book.

ISBN-13: 978-1519797711
ISBN-10: 1519797710

Printed in the United States of America

Neville Goddard (1905-1972) was one of the great spiritual teachers of the 20th century.

This short guide is a compilation of Neville's exceptional advice regarding the mystical birth and meaning of Jesus.

Behold, a virgin shall be with child,
and shall bring forth a son,
and they shall call his name Emmanuel,
which being interpreted is, God with us.
Matthew 1:23

ONE of the most controversial statements in the New Testament concerns the virgin conception and subsequent birth of Jesus, a conception in which man had no part. It's recorded that a virgin conceived a son without the aid of man, then secretly and without effort gave birth to her conception. This is the foundation upon which all Christendom rests. The Christian world is asked to believe this story, for man must believe the unbelievable to fully express the greatness that he is.

Scientifically, we might be inclined to discard the whole Bible as untrue because our reason will not permit us to believe that the virgin birth is physiologically possible, but the Bible is a message of the soul, and must be interpreted psychologically if we're to discover its true symbolism.

We must see this story as a psychological drama rather than a statement of physical fact. In so doing, we'll discover the Bible to be based on a law which – if self-applied – will result in a manifested expression transcending our wildest dreams of accomplishment.

To apply this law of self-expression, we must be schooled in the belief and disciplined to stand upon the platform that "all things are possible to God."

Throughout the centuries we've mistakenly taken symbolic personifications for actual people, allegory for history, the vehicle that conveyed the instruction for the instruction, and the gross first sense for the ultimate sense intended. The ancient Biblical storytellers weren't writing history, but an allegorical picture lesson of certain basic principles that they clothed in the garb of history, and they adapted these symbolic stories to the limited capacity of a most uncritical and credulous people.

In writing this psychological drama,

they've personified the story of the soul as the biography of man.

The difference between the form of the Bible and its substance is as great as the difference between a grain of corn and the life germ within that grain. As our assimilative organs discriminate between food that can be built into our system and food that must be discarded, so do our awakened intuitive faculties discover – beneath allegory and parable – the psychological life-germ of the Bible. And, feeding on this, we too cast off the form that conveyed the message.

The outstanding dramatic dates of the New Testament – namely the birth, death and resurrection of Jesus – were timed and dated to coincide with certain astronomical phenomena. The mystics who recorded this story noticed that, at certain seasons of the year, beneficial changes on Earth coincided with astronomical changes above.

Using these cosmic changes, they've marked the birth and resurrection of

Jesus to convey that the same beneficial changes take place psychologically in the consciousness of man as he follows the Biblical law. Even to those who fail to understand it, the story of Christmas is one of the most beautiful stories ever told. When unfolded in the light of its mystic symbolism, it's revealed as the true birth of every manifestation in the world.

This virgin birth is recorded as having taken place on December 25th, or, as certain secret societies celebrate it, on Christmas Eve at midnight on December 24th. Mystics established this date to mark the birth of Jesus because it was in keeping with the great earthly benefits this astronomical change signifies.

The astronomical observations that prompted the authors of this drama to use these dates were all made in the northern hemisphere. So, from an astronomical point of view, the reverse would be true if seen from the southern latitudes. However, this story was recorded in the north and therefore was based on northern observation.

We discovered very early that the sun played a most important part in our life; that without the sun physical life as we knew it couldn't be. So these most important dates in the story of the life of Jesus are based upon the position of the sun as seen from the earth in the northern latitudes.

After the sun reaches its highest point in the heavens in June it gradually falls southward, taking with it the life of the plant world, so that by December almost all of nature has been stilled. Should the sun continue to fall southward, all nature would be stilled unto death.

However, on December 25th, the sun begins its great move northward, bringing with it the promise of salvation and life anew for the world. Each day, as the sun rises higher in the heavens, we gain confidence in being saved from death by cold and starvation; for we know that as the sun moves northward and crosses the equator all nature will rise again, and be resurrected from its long winter sleep.

Our day is measured from midnight to midnight, and since the visible day begins in the east and ends in the west, the ancients said the day was born of that constellation that occupied the eastern horizon at midnight. On Christmas Eve, or midnight of December 24th, the constellation Virgo is rising on the eastern horizon. So it's recorded that this Son and Savior of the world was born of a virgin.

It's also recorded that this virgin mother was traveling through the night; she stopped at an inn and was given the only available room – which was among the animals – and there in a manger, where the animals fed, the shepherds found the Holy Child.

The animals with which the Holy Virgin was lodged are the holy animals of the zodiac. There, in that constantly moving circle of astronomical animals, stands the Holy Mother – Virgo – and there you will see her every midnight of December 24th, standing on the eastern horizon as the sun, savior of the world, starts its journey northward.

Psychologically, this birth takes place in us on that day when we discover our consciousness to be the sun and savior of our world.

When man knows the significance of this mystical statement, "I am the light of the world," he will realize that his *I AM* – or consciousness – is the symbolic sun of his life, the sun which radiates images upon the screen of space. These images are in the likeness of that which he, as man, is conscious of being. Thus qualities and attributes, which appear to move upon the screen of his world, are really projections of this light from *within* himself.

The numberless unrealized hopes and ambitions of man are the seeds that are buried within the consciousness, or virgin womb, of man. There they remain like the seeds of the earth – held in the frozen waste of winter – waiting for the sun to move northward, or for man to return to the knowledge of who he is. In returning, he moves northward through recognition of his true self by claiming:

I AM the light of the world.
John 9:5

When we discover our consciousness – or *I AM* – to be God, the savior of our world, we'll be as the sun in its northern passage.

All hidden urges and ambitions will then be warmed and stimulated into birth by man's knowledge of his true self. He'll claim that he's that which heretofore he hoped to be. Without the aid of any other, he'll define himself as that which he desires to express. He'll discover that his *I AM* is the symbolic virgin conceiving without the aid of man; that all conceptions of himself – when felt and fixed in consciousness – will be embodied easily as living realities in his world.

Man will one day realize that this whole drama takes place in his consciousness, that his unconditioned consciousness – or *I AM* – is the Virgin Mary desiring to express; that through this law of self-expression he defines himself as that which he desires to express, and that without the help or cooperation of anyone he'll express that which he has consciously claimed and defined himself as being.

He'll then understand why Christmas is fixed on December 25th, while Easter is a movable date; why upon the virgin conception the whole of Christendom rests, that his consciousness is the virgin womb, or bride of the Lord, receiving impressions as self-impregnations, and then – without assistance – embodying these impressions as the expressions of his life.

The stories of the Bible, as you see, contain a powerful challenge to our thinking capacity. The underlying truth – that they're symbolic, psychological dramas and not historical facts –

demands reiteration, inasmuch as it's the only justification for the stories.

Every person automatically expresses that which they're conscious of being.

Without effort or the use of words, at every moment of time we're commanding ourselves to be and to possess that which we're conscious of being and possessing. This changeless principle of expression is dramatized throughout the Bible.

The writers of our sacred books were illuminated mystics, past masters in the art of psychology. In telling the story of the soul, they personified this impersonal principle in the form of a historical document both to preserve it and hide it from the eyes of the uninitiated. Today, those to whom these great treasures have been entrusted – namely the priesthoods of the world – have forgotten that the Bible is a psychological drama representing the consciousness of man. In their blind forgetfulness, they now teach their followers to worship its symbolic characters as men and women who actually lived in time and space. But with a little imagination we may easily retrace the psychological sense in all these stories.

> *And God said,*
> *Let us make man in our image,*
> *after our likeness:*
> *and let them have dominion over the fish of*
> *the sea, and over the fowl of the air,*
> *and over the cattle, and over all the earth,*
> *and over every creeping thing*
> *that creepeth upon the earth.*
> *So God created man in his own image,*
> *in the image of God created he him.*
> Genesis 1:26-27

Here, in the first chapter of the Bible, the ancient teachers laid the foundation that God and man are one, and that man has dominion over all the earth. If God and man are one then God can never be so far off as even to be near, for nearness implies separation. The question then arises: what is God?

God is man's own consciousness, his

awareness, his I AM-ness.

The drama of life is a psychological one in which we bring circumstances to pass by our attitudes rather than by our acts. The cornerstone on which all things are based is man's concept of himself. He acts as he does, and has the experiences that he does, because his concept of himself is what it is, and for no other reason. Had he a different concept of himself, he would act differently and have different experiences.

We, by assuming the feeling of our wish fulfilled, alter our future in harmony with our assumption – for assumptions, though false, if sustained will harden into fact.

When we can see the Bible as a great psychological drama, with all of its characters and actors as the personified qualities and attributes of our own consciousness, then – *and only then* – will the Bible reveal to us the light of its symbolism.

This impersonal principle of life that made all things is personified as God. This Lord God, Creator of Heaven and Earth, is discovered to be our awareness of being. If we were less bound by orthodoxy and more intuitively observant, we couldn't fail to notice in the reading of the Bible that the awareness of being is revealed hundreds of times throughout this literature. To name a few:

I AM hath sent me unto you.
Exodus 3:14

Be still and know that I AM God.
Psalm 46:10

I AM the Lord, and there is none else, there is no God beside me.
Isaiah 45:5

I AM the good shepherd.
John 10:11&14

I AM the door.
John 10:7&9

I AM the resurrection and the life.
John 11:25

I AM the way.
John 14:6

*I AM Alpha and Omega,
the beginning and the end.*
Revelation 21:6 & 22:13

I AM, man's unconditioned awareness of being, is revealed as Lord and Creator of every conditioned state of being.

If man would give up his belief in a God apart from himself, recognize his awareness of being to be God – and this awareness fashions itself in the likeness and image of its conception of itself – he'd transform his world from a barren wasteland to a fertile field of his own liking.

The day man does this he'll know that he and his Father are one, but his Father is greater than he. He'll know that his consciousness of being is one with that which he's conscious of being, but that his unconditioned consciousness of being is *greater* than his conditioned state or conception of himself.

When man discovers his consciousness to be the impersonal power of expression – the power that eternally personifies itself in his conceptions of himself – he'll assume and appropriate that state of consciousness which he desires to express. In so doing he'll *become* that state in expression.

"Ye shall decree a thing and it shall come to pass" can now be told in this manner: you shall become conscious of being or possessing a thing, and you shall express or possess that which you are conscious of being. The law of consciousness is the only law of expression: "*I AM* the way;" "*I AM* the resurrection."

Consciousness is the way, as well as the power, which resurrects and expresses *all* that man will ever be conscious of being.

Turn from the blindness of the uninitiated man – who attempts to express and possess those qualities and things which he's not conscious of being and possessing – and become like the ancient mystics who decreed on the basis of this changeless law. Consciously claim yourself to be that which you seek. Appropriate the consciousness of that which you see. Then you, too, will know the meaning of this:

I became conscious of being it. I'm still conscious of being it. And I shall continue to be conscious of being it until that which I'm conscious of being is perfectly expressed. Yes, I shall decree a thing, and it shall come to pass.

Today, there's so much said about masters, experts and gurus that numerous truth-seekers are being misled by seeking false lights. For a price, most of these pseudo-teachers offer their students initiation into mysteries, promising them guidance and direction. Our weakness for leaders, as well as our worship of idols, makes us easy prey for such schools and teachers.

Good eventually will come to most of these enrolled students. They'll discover, after years of waiting and sacrificing, that they were following a mirage. They'll then become disillusioned in their schools and teachers, and this disappointment will be worth the effort and price they've paid for their fruitless search. They'll then turn from their worship of others, and in so doing discover that which they're seeking isn't to be found in another.

For the Kingdom of Heaven is within.

This realization will be their first real initiation. The lesson learned will be this: there's only one Master and this Master is God, the *I AM* within ourselves.

I AM the Lord thy God, which have brought thee out of the land of Egypt, out of the house of bondage.
Exodus 20:2

I AM – your awareness – is Lord and Master, and besides your awareness there's neither lord nor master. You're Master of all that you'll ever be aware of being.

You know that you are, don't you? *Knowing that you are* is the Lord and Master of that which you know that you are. You could be completely isolated by man by that which you are conscious of being; yet you would, in spite of all human barriers, effortlessly draw to yourself all that you were conscious of being. The man who is conscious of being poor doesn't need the assistance of anyone to express his poverty. The man who is conscious of being sick, although isolated in the most sealed, germ-proof area in the world, would still express sickness.

There's no barrier to God, for God is your awareness of being. Regardless of *what* you're aware of being, you can and do express it without effort. Stop looking for the master to come; He is with you always.

*I AM with you always,
even unto the end of the world.*
Matthew 28:20

Over time you'll know yourself to be many different things, but you need not be anything in particular to know that *you are*. You can, if you so desire, disentangle yourself from the body you wear. In so doing, you realize that you're a faceless, formless awareness and not dependent on the form you now are in your expression. You'll know that *you are*; you'll also discover that this *knowing that you are* is God – the Father – which preceded all that you currently know yourself to be.

There are no special ascended masters. Banish this superstition. *You* simply rise from one level of consciousness to another by mastering it; in so doing you manifest the ascended level, expressing this newly acquired consciousness. Consciousness being Lord and Master, you're the master magician conjuring that which you're now conscious of being. For God (your consciousness) "calleth those things which be not as though they were." Things that aren't now seen will be seen the moment you become *conscious of being that which isn't now seen.*

This rising from one level of consciousness to another is the only ascension that you'll ever experience. No other person can lift you to the level you desire. The power to ascend is within yourself; it's your consciousness. You appropriate the consciousness of the level you desire to express by claiming that you're now expressing such a level. This is the ascension. It's limitless, for you'll never exhaust your capacity to ascend. Turn from the human superstition of ascension, with its belief in masters, to find the only and everlasting Master within yourself.

*Greater is HE that is in you,
than he that is in the world.*
1 John 4:4

Believe this. Don't continue in blindness, following after the mirage of masters. I assure you your search can end only in disappointment:

*Whosoever shall deny ME before men,
him will I also deny before MY Father.*
Matthew 10:33

*Look unto ME, and be ye saved,
all the ends of the earth:
for I AM God, and there is none else.*
Isaiah 45:22

*Thou shalt know no God but ME,
for there is no savior beside ME.*
Hosea 13:4

*Prove ME now herewith,
saith the Lord of hosts,
if I will not open you the windows of heaven,
and pour you out a blessing,
that there shall not be room enough
to receive it.*
Malachi 3:10

Do you believe that the *I AM* is able to do this? Then claim it to be that which you want to see poured out. Claim yourself to be that which you want to be...*and that you shall be*. Not because of masters will it be given to you, but because you have recognized yourself *to be that*: I will give it unto you for *I AM* all things to all.

Some of you still may be inclined to believe that, although we can give it a psychological interpretation, the Bible could be left in its present form and be interpreted literally.

You can't do it.

For this Bible of ours has nothing to do with history. It has no reference to people or to events as you have been taught to believe. The sooner you begin to rub out that historical picture, and a belief in masters apart from yourself, the better. The symbolic stories of the Bible concern themselves exclusively with the power of imagination; they have *nothing* to with historical masters. They're really dramatizations of the technique of prayer, for prayer is the secret to changing your future. The Bible reveals the key by which you may enter a dimensionally larger world for the purpose of changing the conditions of the lesser world in which you live.

In the story of Jesus, he wouldn't permit himself to be called Good Master. He knew that there's but one good, and one Master. He knew this one to be his Father in Heaven, the awareness of being.

Behold, the kingdom of God is within you.
Luke 17:21

Your belief in masters is a confession of your slavery. Only slaves have masters. Change your conception of yourself and you will, without the aid of masters or anyone else, automatically transform your world to conform to your changed conception of yourself.

You're told in the Book of Numbers that there was a time when men were in their own eyes as grasshoppers, and because of this conception of themselves they saw giants in the land. This is as true of man today as it was the day it was recorded. Man's conception of himself is so grasshopper-like that he automatically makes the conditions around about him appear gigantic; in his blindness he cries out for masters to help him fight his giant problems.

Jesus tried to show people that salvation was to be found within them, and warned them not to look for their savior in any other people or places. Jesus not only refused to permit himself to be called Good Master, he warned his followers, "Salute no man along the highway." He made it clear that they shouldn't recognize any authority or superior other than God, the Father. Jesus established the identity of the Father as man's awareness of being.

I and my Father are one.
John 10:30

*If ye loved me, ye would rejoice,
because I said, I go unto the Father:
for my Father is greater than I.*
John 14:28

I AM one with all that I'm conscious of being. *I AM* greater than that which I'm aware of being. The Creator is ever greater than his creation.

> *As Moses lifted up the serpent*
> *in the wilderness, even so must*
> *the Son of man be lifted up.*
> John 3:14

The serpent symbolizes man's present conception of himself as a worm of the dust, living in the wilderness of human confusion. Just as Moses lifted himself from his worm-of-the-dust conception of himself to discover God to be his awareness of being, so must you be lifted up.

> *And God said unto Moses,*
> *I AM THAT I AM: and he said,*
> *Thus shalt thou say unto the children of*
> *Israel, I AM hath sent me unto you.*
> Exodus 3:14

The day you claim as Moses did, that day your claim will blossom in the wilderness. This Lord and Master that you are can and does make all that you're conscious of being appear in your world. You're constantly drawing to yourself that which you're conscious of being. Change your conception of yourself from that of the slave to that of Christ.

Don't be embarrassed to make this claim. Only as you claim, "*I AM* Christ," will you do the works of Christ:

He that believeth on me,
the works that I do shall he do also;
and greater works than these shall he do;
because I go unto my Father.
John 14:12

Let this mind be in you,
which was also in Christ Jesus:
Who, being in the form of God,
thought it not robbery to be equal with God.
Philippians 2:5-6

Jesus knew that anyone who dared to claim himself to be Christ would automatically assume the capacities to express the works of his conception of Christ.

Jesus also knew that the exclusive use of this principle of expression wasn't given to him alone. He constantly referred to his Father in Heaven. He stated that his works would not only be equaled, but that they'd be surpassed by that man who dared to conceive himself to be greater than Jesus had conceived himself to be.

Jesus, in stating that he and his Father were one but that his Father was greater than he, revealed his awareness (Father) to be one with that which he was aware of being. You and your conception of yourself are one. You are, and always will be, greater than any conception you have of yourself.

Man fails to do the works of Jesus Christ because he attempts to accomplish them from his present level of consciousness. You'll never transcend your present accomplishments through sacrifice and struggle. Your present level of consciousness will only be transcended as you *drop* the present state and rise to a higher level.

You rise to a higher level of consciousness by taking your attention away from your present limitations and placing it instead upon that which you desire to be. Don't attempt this just by daydreaming or wishful thinking, but in a more holistic manner: *actually claim yourself to be the thing desired.*

I AM that. No sacrifice, no diet, no human tricks. All that is asked of you is to *accept* your desire.

If you dare claim it, you will express it. Meditate on these:

Every one that thirsteth, come ye to the waters, and he that hath no money; come ye, buy, and eat; yea, come, buy wine and milk without money and without price.
Isaiah 55:1

Not by might, nor by power, but by my spirit.
Zechariah 4:6

Ask, and it shall be given you;
seek, and ye shall find;
knock, and it shall be opened unto you.
Matthew 7:7

I AM the Lord thy God,
which brought thee out of the land of Egypt:
open thy mouth wide, and I will fill it.
Psalm 81:10

And all things, whatsoever ye shall ask in
prayer, believing, ye shall receive.
Matthew 21:22

Hitherto have ye asked nothing in my name:
ask, and ye shall receive,
that your joy may be full.
John 16:24

If ye shall ask any thing in my name,
I will do it.
John 14:14

The works are finished.

All that's required of you to let these qualities into expression is the claim: *I AM* that.

Claim yourself to be that which you desire to be and that you shall be. Expressions follow the impressions, they do not precede them. Proof that you are will follow the claim that you are, it will not precede it.

"Leave all and follow Me" is a double invitation to you. First, it invites you to *turn completely away* from all problems, and then it calls upon you to *continue walking in the claim* that you are that which you desire to be. Don't be Lot's wife, who looks back and becomes salted, preserved in the dead past. Be Lot, who doesn't look back, but who keeps his vision focused upon the Promised Land, the thing desired.

Do this and you'll know that you've found the Master, making the unseen the seen through the command, *"I AM THAT."*

FREQUENTLY ASKED
QUESTIONS AND ANSWERS

If Jesus was a fictional character created by Biblical writers for the purpose of illustrating certain psychological dramas, how do you account for the fact that he and his philosophy are mentioned in the nonreligious and non-Christian history of those times? Weren't Pontius Pilate and Herod real flesh and blood Roman officials in those days?

The story of Jesus is the identical story as that of the Hindu savior, Krishna. They're the same psychological characters. Both were supposed to have been born of virgin mothers. The rulers of the time sought to destroy them when they were children. Both healed the sick, resurrected the dead, taught the gospel of love and died a martyr's death for mankind. Hindus and Christians alike believe their savior to be God made man.

Today people quote Socrates, yet the only proof that Socrates ever existed is in the works of Plato. It's said that Socrates drank hemlock – but I ask you, who is Socrates?

I once quoted a line from Shakespeare and a lady said to me, "But Hamlet said that."

Hamlet never said it – Shakespeare wrote the lines and put the words in the mouth of a character he created and named Hamlet.

Saint Augustine once said, "That which is now called the Christian religion existed among the ancients. They began to call Christianity the true religion, yet it never existed."

Who wrote the Bible?

The Bible was written by intelligent men who used solar and phallic myths to reveal psychological truths. But we've mistaken their allegory for history and therefore failed to see their true message.

It's strange, but when the Bible was launched upon the world – and acceptance seemed to be in sight – the great Alexandria Library was burnt to the ground, leaving no record as to how the Bible came into being. Few people can read other languages, so they cannot compare their beliefs with others. Our churches don't encourage us to compare.

How many of the millions who accept the Bible as fact ever question it? Believing it's the word of God, they blindly accept the words, and thus lose the essence they contain. Having accepted the vehicle they don't understand what the vehicle conveys.

What's your technique for prayer?

It starts with desire. For desire is the mainspring of action. You must know and define your objective; then condense it into a sensation that implies fulfillment.

When your desire is clearly defined, immobilize your physical body and experience – in your imagination – the action that implies its fulfillment. Repeat this act over and over again, until it has the vividness and feeling of reality.

Or condense your desire into a single phrase that implies fulfillment, such as, "Thank you, Father," "Isn't it wonderful," or "It's finished."

Repeat that condensed phrase or action in your imagination over and over again. Then either wake from that state, or slip off into the deep. It doesn't matter, for the act is done when you completely accept it as being finished in that sleepy, drowsy state.

Why do those who work hard in metaphysics always seem to lack?

Because they haven't really applied metaphysics.

I'm not speaking of a mamby-pamby approach to life, but a daily application of the law of consciousness. When you appropriate your good, there's no need for a person, or state, to act as a medium through which your good will come.

Living in this modern world, money is needed in my everyday life. If I invite you to lunch tomorrow, I must pick up the check. When I leave the hotel, I must pay the bill. In order to take the train back to New York my railway fare must be paid. I need money and it has to be there. I'm not going to say, "God knows best, and He knows I need money." Rather, I'll appropriate the money as though it were!

We must live boldly! We must go through life as though we possess what we want to possess. Don't think that because you helped another, someone outside of you saw your good works and will give you something to ease your burden. There's no one to do it for you. You, yourself, must go boldly on appropriating what your Father has already given you.

Is it possible to imagine several things at the same time, or should I confine my imagining to one desire?

Personally, I like to confine my imaginal act to a single thought, but that doesn't mean I'll stop there. During the course of a day I may imagine many things. But instead of imagining lots of small things, I'd suggest that you imagine something so big it includes all the little things. Instead of imagining wealth, health and friends, imagine being ecstatic. You couldn't be ecstatic and be in pain. You couldn't be ecstatic and be threatened with a dispossession notice. You couldn't be ecstatic if you weren't enjoying a full measure of friendship and love.

What would the feeling be like were you ecstatic without knowing what had happened to produce your ecstasy? Reduce the idea of ecstasy to the single sensation, "Isn't it wonderful!"

Don't allow the conscious, reasoning mind to ask why, because if it does it'll start to look for visible causes, and then the sensation will be lost. Rather, repeat over and over again, "Isn't it wonderful!" Suspend judgment as to what's wonderful.

Catch the one sensation of the wonder of it all and things will happen to bear witness to the truth of this sensation. And I promise you, it'll include all the little things.

"*Assume you are what you want to be. Walk in that assumption and it will harden into fact.*"

Part of the
NEVILLE EXPLAINS THE BIBLE
Series

Other books in the series include:

RELAX MORE, TRY LESS

MANIFESTING MIRACLES

MINDFUL MANIFESTATION

FEELING IS THE SECRET

FREEDOM FOR ALL

PRAYER

THE POWER OF AWARENESS

MEDITATION

Taught by Neville Goddard

Edited by Tim Grimes

For more information visit:

www.radicalcounselor.com

Made in the USA
San Bernardino, CA
24 May 2019